PREPARING TO WIN IN THE FIRST QUARTER

CHERNEVA THOMAS JOHNSON

Copyright © 2024

All Rights Reserved.

DEDICATION

This book is dedicated to my beloved son, Tabaius Anderson, who would have been 21 years old. Pursuing our family's dreams without you has been one of my greatest challenges, yet your memory remains my source of strength.

I want you to know that I love you deeply and will never forget you. Your absence has fueled my determination to keep moving forward.

Love always, Tabaius Anderson.

ACKNOWLEDGMENT

First and foremost, I want to Thank God, who has been my unwavering guide through every situation. His faithfulness has never wavered, always showing me a way forward, no matter the obstacles. Choosing to trust in Him has been my greatest strength.

To my children, you are my inspiration and my purpose. You are the reason I push forward every day, reaching for the stars with a determination to soar. As I reflect on my journey, I see how deeply you motivate me to set the bar high, striving to be the best mother I can be. I pray that you surpass my achievements and reach even greater heights.

CONTENTS

Dedication i
Acknowledgment ii
About The Author iv
Introduction: The Journey To Homeownership v
My Story: Faith, Family, And Overcoming Obstacles .. 1
Facing Health Challenges: God's Miracles At Work ... 3
Why I Want To Help You: Passion Fueled By Purpose ... 5
Steps To Homeownership: A Detailed Roadmap 7
Building Generational Wealth: Leaving A Legacy For Your Family 13
Faith And Perseverance: Overcoming Setbacks 14
Conclusion: Your Journey Begins Today 15
Appendix: Helpful Resources For First-Time Homebuyers 16
Scriptures Referenced In This Guide: 17

About The Author

Cherneva Thomas is a distinguished author, Realtor, and college graduate. With a passion for both real estate and storytelling, she has successfully blended her expertise in the housing market with her creative writing skills.

As a Realtor, Cherneva is known for her innovative approach and dedication to helping clients find their perfect homes. Her academic background, coupled with her hands-on experience, makes her a well-rounded professional who excels in every endeavor she undertakes. Cherneva's commitment to excellence is evident in her work, whether she's guiding clients through real estate transactions or crafting compelling narratives in her writing.

Introduction: The Journey To Homeownership

Have you ever found yourself passionately declaring, "This is the year I'll buy a home!" only to realize that another year has passed, and that goal still seems distant? If that's the case, then you're not alone.

I'm Cherneva Thomas Johnson, and I know firsthand the empowerment that comes with owning a home. Watching my grandparents rent their entire lives was a powerful lesson for me. After my grandfather passed, my uncle bought a house for my grandmother. Sadly, she didn't live long enough to enjoy it, and neither of them experienced the security and pride of homeownership during their lifetime.

Homeownership represents far more than just a place to live. It symbolizes generational wealth, stability, and a foundation that provides for future success. When hard times come, owning a home gives you the equity to leverage your property for financial support. Sadly, like many others, my grandparents didn't understand the value and opportunity homeownership could have afforded them.

This is the cycle we will break together, and this year, we will **prepare to win in the first quarter of your homeownership journey**!

The Bible says in *Hosea 4:6,*

"My people are destroyed for lack of knowledge."

Too many people fail to reach their dreams, not because they lack desire but because they lack information and the right tools to succeed. The dream of owning a home may seem distant for you now, but I'm here to tell you that with the right preparation, that dream is within your grasp. My mission is to help you gain the knowledge needed to turn your dream into a reality. I understand what you are going through because I've been in your shoes—and I am confident you can succeed.

Owning a home is a multi-step journey that may feel overwhelming at times, but it's important to remember that.

"God's plan for us is to prosper and not to harm u."

(*Jeremiah 29:11*).

When we step out in faith, we trust that God will guide us at each step of the process. The knowledge I'm about to share with you will equip you to take those steps with confidence.

My Story: Faith, Family, And Overcoming Obstacles

Allow me to share a bit of my story, one filled with faith, challenges, and triumphs. I am a mother of seven, although one of my children has passed away and is now in Heaven.

Today, I have six children who serve as my driving force. As a mother, I understand what it means to face difficulties, to want more for your family but not always know how to achieve it. However, I also know that **God makes a way when there seems to be no way**.

Coming from a rough background, my mother raised us as a single parent in financial hardship. Yet, the one thing she never lacked was **an unshakable faith in God**. Her love for the Lord remained unwavering, and she passed that deep faith to me and my siblings. Even when life's storms raged around us, she continued to trust in God's provision. This foundation of faith has been my guiding light throughout my own journey.

At a young age, I dropped out of school, and life took an unexpected turn when I became pregnant. But God had other plans for me. By His grace, I was able to return to school and graduate. I went on to college, eventually got married, and my husband and I purchased our first home. Unfortunately, we bought it through owner financing—a process I didn't fully understand at the time. Later, during our divorce, I gave up the house, unaware that it was legally mine. It wasn't until later that I learned the true power and responsibility of property ownership.

That moment was a turning point in my life. It ignited a deep passion within me to better understand homeownership better and help others avoid the same mistakes. Today, my purpose is to guide others through the process of owning a home and securing a stable, prosperous future for their families. This is not just a job for me; it's a calling, and it aligns with **God's purpose for my life**.

In *Proverbs 16:9*, the Bible says,

"In their hearts humans plan their course, but the Lord establishes their steps."

Every experience I've had has been part of God's preparation for my mission to help others.

FACING HEALTH CHALLENGES: GOD'S MIRACLES AT WORK

Life often tests your strength, and it is through these tests that we discover God's grace and power. After buying our first home, I was diagnosed with a rare kidney disease that led to nine years of dialysis. During that time, I became pregnant with my son, and doctors strongly recommended I terminate the pregnancy. They believed my body couldn't handle the strain. But as a woman of **faith**, I knew abortion was not an option.

The doctors warned that my son would face serious developmental challenges, predicting he wouldn't walk or have a normal life. But God is a healer. Today, my son is thriving, with none of the limitations they had predicted.

As it says in *2 Corinthians 5:7,*

"For we walk by faith, not by sight."

There are moments when the facts before you do not align with the faith in your heart. But when we trust God, He always makes a way, even when the situation seems impossible.

During my illness, I faced additional challenges. High doses of prednisone, a powerful steroid, blurred my vision and left me unable to focus, making it impossible for me to pass my real estate exam. Despite the physical limitations, I wasn't discouraged. I knew God had a plan. The doctors later confirmed that the medication was preventing me from concentrating, but I continued to trust in the Lord's timing.

After those difficult years, God spoke to me and said, "It's time." I retook the real estate exam and passed! That moment was a personal victory but also a victory for everyone who had prayed with me through my struggles. It's a reminder of the truth found in *Isaiah 40:31*,

"But those who hope in the Lord will renew their strength. They will soar on wings like eagles; they will run and not grow weary; they will walk and not be faint."

God's timing is perfect, and He always restores what we lose in life's battles.

Not only did I gain the strength to overcome my health challenges, but my son also surpassed every expectation. Today, I stand as a living testament to the **miracle-working power of God**, and I believe that God wants to do the same in your life. No matter what obstacles stand in your way—whether they are financial, emotional, or physical—God has a plan to bring you through.

In *Romans 8:28*, we are reminded,

"And we know that in all things God works for the good of those who love him, who have been called according to his purpose."

Everything you face can be turned around for your good if you trust in Him.

WHY I WANT TO HELP YOU: PASSION FUELED BY PURPOSE

Over the years, I have witnessed how a **lack of knowledge** can destroy opportunities. In one neighborhood I lived in, many families were already struggling with subpar living conditions. The city council allowed a scrapyard to be built in the middle of the community, bringing pests and hazardous conditions to their homes. The residents—elderly, families with young children, and hardworking individuals—deserved better. They lacked the knowledge and resources to move into healthier, more secure homes.

This experience ignited my passion to help others escape similar situations. **Homeownership** not only provides a roof over your head; it protects your family, offers dignity, and opens doors to financial freedom. The Bible says in *Proverbs 24:3-4,*

"By wisdom a house is built, and through understanding, it is established; through knowledge, its rooms are filled with rare and beautiful treasures."

I want to empower you with wisdom and knowledge to build that house and secure your future.

As a mother and a woman of faith, I believe that we are called to be **stewards of the resources** God gives us. When you own a home, you are not only taking care of your own needs but also creating a legacy for your children. Owning property is one of the most powerful ways to build wealth over time, and it's an opportunity that I believe every family deserves to have.

Let's talk about how we can make this happen for you. This isn't just about getting a mortgage and buying a house. It's about creating a stable foundation for your future, **breaking the chains of poverty**, and setting your family on the path to financial independence. Owning a home is a key part of that journey.

STEPS TO HOMEOWNERSHIP: A DETAILED ROADMAP

Owning a home can seem overwhelming, but when you break it down into manageable steps, the path becomes much clearer. Let's walk through these essential steps together so that you can confidently **prepare to win.**

1. *Credit Score: Your Financial Foundation*

Your credit score is more than just a number; it is a **reflection of your financial responsibility.** Mortgage lenders rely on your score to determine your risk as a borrower. The three major credit bureaus—Equifax, Experian, and TransUnion—each calculate your score slightly differently, but lenders generally require a minimum score of 580 to qualify for a mortgage. At this level, you will face higher interest rates. For better rates and terms, aim for a score of *620 or higher.*

Improving your credit score takes time, but it's worth the effort. Start by reviewing your credit report for any errors, paying down existing debt, and ensuring all bills are paid on time. Consider seeking guidance from a **credit counselor** if you feel overwhelmed, but remember—improving your credit is possible with **discipline** and patience.

In *Luke 16:10*, the Bible says,

> *"Whoever can be trusted with very little can also be trusted with much."*

Taking small, consistent steps toward improving your credit will open the door to greater financial opportunities down the road.

2. Saving for a Down Payment: Preparing for Your Investment

The size of your down payment will vary depending on the type of loan you choose. Most first-time buyers should aim for 3.5% to 5% of the home's purchase price, although some programs, such as VA loans for veterans, offer no down payment options. Start by creating a budget and **setting aside savings** specifically for your down payment.

In *Proverbs 21:20*, the Bible tells us,

> *"The wise store up choice food and olive oil, but fools gulp theirs down."*

Wise financial planning will ensure you're ready to seize the opportunity when the right home comes along. You might also explore down payment assistance programs, many of which are available for first-time buyers.

3. Debt-to-Income Ratio: Managing Your Finances Wisely

Lenders assess your debt-to-income (DTI) ratio to evaluate whether you can afford a mortgage. Your DTI is the percentage of your monthly income that goes toward paying debts, including credit cards, car loans, and student loans. The lower your DTI, the better your chances of qualifying for a mortgage with favorable terms. Most lenders look for a DTI of 43% or less.

To improve your DTI, start by paying down your debts, particularly high-interest debts like credit cards. If necessary, consider consolidating your loans to lower your monthly payments and reduce your interest rates.

In *Romans 13:8*, the Bible reminds us,

"Let no debt remain outstanding, except the continuing debt to love one another."

Being a good steward of your financial obligations will help you achieve the stability needed to own a home.

Remember, **God wants us to prosper**, but we also have a responsibility to manage our finances wisely. This includes understanding the importance of budgeting, reducing debt, and living within our means as we work toward our goal of homeownership.

4. *Pre-Approval for a Mortgage: Knowing Your Buying Power*

Before you start searching for homes, it's essential to get pre-approved for a mortgage. A pre-approval letter from a lender not only shows sellers that you're a serious buyer but also helps you understand exactly how much house you can afford. The lender will evaluate your financial history, income, credit score, and DTI to determine your loan eligibility.

This is a crucial step because it gives you a clear picture of your buying power and helps you set realistic expectations.

In *Habakkuk 2:2-3*, the Bible advises,

"Write the vision and make it plain on tablets, that he may run who reads it."

By securing pre-approval, you are essentially writing down your vision for homeownership in clear terms, which allows you to move forward confidently.

5. *Choosing the Right Home: Finding a Place to Plant Roots*

Once you've secured financing, the next step is finding the right home. This is where the journey becomes exciting but also requires wisdom and discernment. Consider your family's needs, including the number of bedrooms, location, and neighborhood. Take your time to research school districts, nearby amenities, and future developments in the area. Your home is more than just a financial investment; it's where your family will grow and create memories.

Ask God for guidance during this process.

In *Proverbs 3:5-6*, we are reminded to

"Trust in the Lord with all your heart and lean not on your own understanding; in all your ways submit to him,

and he will make your paths straight."

Trust that God will guide you to the right home that meets your family's needs and aligns with your financial goals.

6. *The Home Inspection: Ensuring a Solid Foundation*

Once you've found the home of your dreams, it's essential to hire a professional home inspector. The inspection will reveal any potential problems with the property, such as structural issues, plumbing problems, or roof damage. While this step might seem like an added expense, it's crucial to ensure you're making a wise investment.

In *Luke 14:28*, the Bible tells us,

"Suppose one of you wants to build a tower. Won't you first sit down and estimate the cost to see if you have enough money to complete it?"

A home inspection allows you to count the cost and make sure you're prepared for any repairs or maintenance that may be needed. It's always better to know about potential issues upfront than to be surprised after closing.

7. *Closing the Deal: Sealing Your Commitment*

After the inspection, negotiations, and finalizing of your loan, you'll reach the closing stage. At closing, you'll sign the final documents, pay closing costs, and officially take ownership of your new home. This is the moment you've been working toward—the moment when your dream of homeownership becomes a reality.

In *Deuteronomy 28:12*, the Bible says,

"The Lord will open the heavens, the storehouse of his bounty, to send rain on your land in season and to bless all the work of your hands."

Closing day is a testament to the blessings of hard work, faith, and careful preparation. It's a day to celebrate the fulfillment of a dream, knowing that with God's guidance, you have successfully prepared to win.

BUILDING GENERATIONAL WEALTH: LEAVING A LEGACY FOR YOUR FAMILY

One of the greatest blessings of homeownership is the ability to create generational wealth. Your home is not just a place to live; it's an asset that can be passed down to your children and grandchildren. By owning a home, you're laying the foundation for financial stability that will benefit future generations.

In *Proverbs 13:22*, the Bible says,

"A good person leaves an inheritance for their children's children."

As homeowners, we have the opportunity to leave a lasting legacy for our families. By building equity in your home, you can ensure that your children start their adult lives with a financial advantage. This is part of **God's plan for prosperity**, not just for you but for your descendants.

FAITH AND PERSEVERANCE: OVERCOMING SETBACKS

The journey to homeownership is not always smooth. There may be setbacks along the way, such as financial challenges, unexpected repairs, or difficulties securing a loan. But remember, **God is with you every step of the way**. He sees your efforts and knows your heart's desire for a stable home.

In *James 1:3-4*, the Bible reminds us,

"Because you know that the testing of your faith produces perseverance. Let perseverance finish its work so that you may be mature and complete, not lacking anything."

Every challenge you face is an opportunity for growth and perseverance. Trust in God's timing and know that He is preparing you for the blessing of homeownership.

CONCLUSION: YOUR JOURNEY BEGINS TODAY

As you embark on this journey, remember that homeownership is not just about the physical property you'll acquire; it's about the spiritual and financial foundation you'll build for your family. By following the steps outlined in this guide, you're preparing to win in the first quarter of your homeownership journey.

In *Philippians 4:13*, the Bible says,

"I can do all things through Christ who strengthens me."

With faith, determination, and the right knowledge, you have everything you need to achieve your dream of owning a home. **God is with you**, and He will guide you through each step of the process.

This is your year. This is your moment. Together, we will **prepare to win**!

Appendix:
Helpful Resources
For First-Time Homebuyers

1. **HUD Approved Housing Counseling Agencies**
   These agencies offer free or low-cost advice on buying a home, foreclosure avoidance, credit issues, and more.

2. **FHA Loans**
   The Federal Housing Administration (FHA) offers loans with lower down payment requirements, making homeownership accessible to more people.

3. **VA Loans**
   Veterans and active military members can take advantage of VA loans, which often have no down payment requirements.

4. **First-Time Homebuyer Grants**
   Many local and state programs offer grants to help first-time buyers with down payments and closing costs.

SCRIPTURES REFERENCED IN THIS GUIDE:

1. Hosea 4:6 – "My people are destroyed for lack of knowledge."
2. Jeremiah 29:11 – "For I know the plans I have for you... plans to prosper you and not to harm you plans to give you hope and a future."
3. 2 Corinthians 5:7 – "For we walk by faith, not by sight."
4. Isaiah 40:31 – "But those who hope in the Lord will renew their strength."
5. Proverbs 24:3-4 – "By wisdom a house is built, and through understanding, it is established."
6. Luke 16:10 – "Whoever can be trusted with very little can also be trusted with much."
7. Habakkuk 2:2-3 – "Write the vision and make it plain on tablets."
8. Proverbs 21:20 – "The wise store up choice food and olive oil."
9. Romans 13:8 – "Let no debt remain outstanding."
10. James 1:3-4 – "The testing of your faith produces perseverance."
11. Philippians 4:13 – "I can do all things through Christ who strengthens me."

Made in the USA
Middletown, DE
17 January 2025